Full of Beans!

Best-Ever Canned Baked Bean Recipes

BY

Christina Tosch

Copyright 2021 Christina Tosch

Copyright Notes

This Book may not be reproduced, in part or in whole, without explicit permission and agreement by the Author by any means. This includes but is not limited to print, electronic media, scanning, photocopying or file sharing.

The Author has made every effort to ensure accuracy of information in the Book but assumes no responsibility should personal or commercial damage arise in the case of misinterpretation or misunderstanding. All suggestions, instructions and guidelines expressed in the Book are meant for informational purposes only, and the Reader assumes any and all risk when following said information.

Table of Contents

Introduction 6

Lite Bites and Mains 8

    Bacon and Avocado Topped Baked Bean Waffles 9

    Baked Bean Curry 12

    Baked Bean Falafel 14

    Baked Bean Lasagna 17

    Baked Beans Sloppy Joes 20

    Baked Bean Shakshuka 22

    BBQ Chicken and Bean Tostadas 25

    Bean, Bacon, and Sausage Hand Pies 28

    Beef and Baked Bean Cottage Pie 31

    Beefy Bean Meatloaf 35

    Budget Baked Bean Pasta 38

    Cheesy Bean Pastry Pockets 40

    Chili Bean Tortilla Soup 42

    Coq Au Vin with Baked Beans 44

Country Ham and Bean Stew 47

Hot Dog Pie 49

Lamb and Bean Casserole 51

Meat-Free Baked Bean Meatball Sub 53

New England-Inspired Baked Bean Soup 55

Pizza Margherita with Baked Beans 57

Potato-Topped Meatballs and Baked Beans 59

Skillet Saltfish, Veggies and Baked Beans 61

Slow-Cooked Paprika Pork, Beans, and Roasted Tomatoes 64

Slow Cooker Chicken and Baked Bean Casserole 66

Spanish-Style Baked Bean Omelet 68

Spicy Baked Bean Tuna Toast Topper 71

Spicy Baked Bean Jambalaya 74

Steak and Baked Bean Stroganoff Pie 76

The Big Breakfast Baked Bean Bake 79

Veggie Cowboy Pie 82

Sides 84

Baked Bean Fritters 85

Baked Bean Mexican-Style Stuffed Bell Peppers 88

BBQ Baked Beans 91

Maple Baked Beans 93

Peach Baked Beans 95

Ratatouille with Baked Beans 98

Slow Cooker Boozy Bourbon Baked Beans with Bacon 101

Spicy Beans and Rice 104

Sweet Corn and Baked Bean Salsa 106

Sweet 'n Sour Beans 108

Author's Afterthoughts 111

About the Author 112

Introduction

Canned baked beans are the perfect ingredient for all sorts of recipes.

Although their name suggests they are baked, most baked beans are stewed in a tomato sauce and are made with navy beans or haricot beans.

Canned baked beans are a store-cupboard food staple. They are quick to prepare, packed full of protein and fiber, and better yet, easy on the pocket.

Did you know?

1 cup of baked beans is equivalent to 1½ servings of veggies.

Baked beans are not only low in fat but also super low in saturated fats.

Baked beans also contain essential minerals, including zinc and iron, and are a valuable source of B vitamins.

Baked beans can play a vital role in ensuring your family enjoys a healthy and balanced diet, especially if you choose baked beans low in salt and sugar.

From pasta to pizza and pies, curry to casseroles, and shakshuka to soups, make sure your family recipes are full of beans!

Lite Bites and Mains

Bacon and Avocado Topped Baked Bean Waffles

Who says baked beans aren't fancy? And here, they are the star of the show for tasty waffles topped with crisp bacon and slices of avocado.

Servings: 2

Total Time: 30mins

Ingredients:

- 2 eggs (separated)
- ⅗ cup plain flour
- ¼ tsp bicarbonate of soda
- ¾ ounce butter (softened)
- 1¼ cups milk
- 1 (14½ ounces) can baked beans (divided)
- 2 strips bacon
- ½ avocado (peeled, pitted, and sliced)

Directions:

For the batter, whisk the egg whites until peaks begin to form.

In a larger bowl, combine the flour with the bicarb.

Create a well in the middle of the flour mixture and add the yolks followed by the melted butter. Fold in the egg whites along with the milk.

Drain the sauce from half a can of the beans, and add the drained beans to the batter. Discard the sauce.

Using your waffle maker, prepare the waffles according to the manufacturer's directions.

In a skillet, cook the bacon until crisp.

Add the remaining beans to a small pan, and heat through.

Serve the waffles topped with the bacon, beans, and slices of avocado.

Serve and enjoy.

Baked Bean Curry

Are you craving a curry but looking for a quick and easy recipe for it? Then, this baked bean curry is the solution. Serve over a jacket potato or on a bed of boiled rice with a portion of naan bread.

Servings: 2

Total Time: 25mins

Ingredients:

- Oil (for frying)
- 1 medium onion (peeled and chopped)
- 1 clove garlic (peeled and crushed)
- 1 thumb-size piece fresh ginger (peeled and crushed)
- Fresh chili (chopped, to taste)
- 1 tsp cumin
- 1 tsp dried coriander
- 1 (14½ ounces) can baked beans
- 1 (14½ ounces) chopped tomatoes

Directions:

Heat a splash of oil in a frying pan.

Add the onion, garlic, and ginger to the pan, and fry until the onion is translucent.

Next, add the chili, cumin, and coriander and fry for 60 seconds.

Stir in the beans, followed by the canned tomatoes.

Simmer the mixture on moderate heat for approximately 15 minutes, until hot.

Serve with jacket potato for a lite bite or over boiled rice with naan bread, as a main.

Baked Bean Falafel

Are you craving falafel but fresh out of chickpeas? Instead, why not make use of those canned baked beans lurking in the back of your store-cupboard!

Servings: 4

Total Time: 45mins

Ingredients:

Falafel:

- 4 (14½ ounces) cans baked beans
- 1 large egg
- 6 cloves garlic (peeled and crushed)
- 1 large onion (peeled and chopped)
- 1 tsp salt
- 1 tsp chili powder
- 1 tbsp ground coriander
- 1 tbsp ground cumin
- 4¼ ounces chickpea flour
- 1 handful fresh parsley (finely chopped)
- Nonstick cooking oil spray

Sauce:

- 1 clove garlic (peeled and grated)
- 1 tsp salt
- 4 tbsp mayonnaise
- 1 squeeze fresh lemon juice
- 1 tbsp fresh parsley (chopped)
- 2 tbsp Sriracha sauce

Directions:

First, drain the baked beans, and set the sauce aside.

Rinse the baked beans, leaving them to drain.

Add the drained beans and egg to a food blender and process to a smooth paste consistency.

Transfer the mixture to a bowl.

Add the garlic, onion, salt, chili powder, coriander, and cumin.

Next, add the flour, mix to combine and create a fairly wet mixture.

Preheat the main oven to 390 degrees F. Liberally grease a large baking tray.

With wet hands, create 20-24 even size balls from the mixture and arrange the balls in a single layer on the prepared tray.

Spray the balls with nonstick cooking oil spray and bake in the preheated oven for 25-30 minutes, flipping them over halfway through cooking.

To prepare the sauce: In a bowl, combine the garlic with the salt, mayonnaise, freshly squeezed lemon juice, parsley, and Sriracha. Add 5¼ ounces of the bean juice set aside in Step 1, and stir to incorporate. Put the mixture to one side.

Serve the falafel with the sauce.

Baked Bean Lasagna

This pocket-friendly budget lasagna is a meat-free alternative to a classic Italian dish. Serve with a crisp green salad or a slice of garlic bread.

Servings: 4

Total Time: 55mins

I

Ingredients:

- Splash of oil
- 1 onion (peeled and chopped small)
- 2 cloves garlic (peeled and chopped small)
- 1 red pepper (seeded and cut into small slices)
- 1 (14½ ounces) can baked beans
- 1 (14½ ounces) can chopped tomatoes
- 1 tsp mixed herbs

Sauce:

- 1¾ tbsp butter
- 3¼ tbsp plain flour
- 1¼ cups whole milk
- 3 ounces cheese (grated)
- 1 tsp mustard
- 10 sheets lasagna
- Freshly ground black pepper (to season)

Directions:

In a skillet, heat a splash of oil and cook the onion with the garlic and red pepper until softened.

Add the baked beans and chopped tomatoes to the pan. Stir in the mixed herbs and put to one side.

In a second pan, prepare the cheese sauce. First, melt the butter, and a little at a time, add the flour to create a smooth paste.

While stirring, gradually add the milk to create a smooth sauce. Once the sauce begins to bubble and thicken, stir in the grated cheese, allowing it to melt. Remove the pan from the heat.

Preheat the main oven to 355 degrees F.

Add ⅓ of the bean mixture to an ovenproof dish.

Top with half of the lasagna sheets and then more of the bean mixture. Add half of the cheese sauce.

Add another layer of lasagna sheets followed by the remaining cheese sauce.

Scatter over some grated cheese.

Bake in the oven until golden and bubbling for 40-45 minutes.

Serve and enjoy.

Baked Beans Sloppy Joes

This is hands-down the best Sloppy Joe recipe ever. Better yet, you can prepare a meal that is ready from pan to plate in only 30 minutes. That's what we call fast food!

Servings: 6

Total Time: 30mins

Ingredients:

- Splash of oil
- 1 pound 2 ounces lean minced beef
- ½ red capsicum (seeded and chopped)
- 1 onion (peeled and chopped)
- 1 (14½ ounces) can baked beans
- ¼ cup store-bought BBQ sauce
- ¼ cup water
- 6 hamburger buns
- 1 red onion (peeled and sliced into rings)

Directions:

Add a splash of oil to a skillet and heat.

Stir in the minced beef, and over moderate to high heat, brown the meat. Using the back of a wooden spoon, break the meat up as it cooks.

Add the red capsicum and onion, and continue to cook for 2-3 minutes.

Stir in the baked beans, and add the BBQ sauce along with ¼ cup water. Bring the mixture to boil before reducing to a simmer. Simmer for 4-6 minutes, or until the meat is cooked through.

Split the hamburger buns and toast.

Spoon the meat onto the bottom half of the buns, top with red onion rings followed by the remaining bun half.

Baked Bean Shakshuka

This simple one-pan Middle Eastern and North African-inspired dish makes a hearty meal for breakfast or brunch.

Servings: 4

Total Time: 45mins

Ingredients:

- 1 tbsp olive oil
- 1 red onion (peeled and finely sliced)
- 1 clove garlic (peeled and crushed)
- 1 yellow bell pepper (seeded and sliced into strips)
- 1 tbsp sweet smoked paprika
- 1 (14½ ounces) can cherry tomatoes
- 1 (14½ ounces) can baked beans
- 4 large eggs
- 1 small handful fresh parsley (chopped, to garnish)
- 1 tsp dried chili flakes (to garnish)
- Flatbread (toasted, to serve, optional)

Directions:

Heat the oil in a large skillet.

Add the onion and the garlic to the pan, and cook until just softened.

Next, add the yellow pepper strips and sweet smoked paprika, and cook for an additional 5 minutes.

Stir in the cherry tomatoes along with the baked beans and combine.

Simmer the mixture over moderate heat, while occasionally stirring, for 10 minutes.

Using the back of a spoon, create 4 small wells in the mixture.

Crack an egg into each well and over a gentle heat, cook for 2-3 minutes, until the whites set, and the yolks are a little runny.

Garnish with chopped parsley and dried chili flakes.

Serve the shakshuka with toasted flatbread.

BBQ Chicken and Bean Tostadas

It's time to put leftover cooked chicken to good use and whip up a batch of these BBQ bean chicken tostadas.

Servings: 4

Total Time: 35mins

Ingredients:

- 2 tbsp freshly squeezed lemon juice
- 2 tbsp full-fat mayonnaise
- 1 tbsp light brown sugar
- ⅛ tsp black pepper
- 2 cups coleslaw mix
- 2 green onions (thinly sliced)
- 1 cup canned baked beans
- 2⅔ cups leftover, cooked chicken (shredded)
- ⅔ cup store-bought BBQ sauce
- 8 tostada shells
- 1 cup smoked Cheddar cheese (shredded)

Directions:

Preheat your broiler.

In a bowl, combine the lemon juice, mayonnaise, brown sugar, and black pepper, and toss with the coleslaw mix and green onions. Transfer to the fridge until you are ready to serve.

Add the baked beans to a pan, and using a potato masher, mash until lump-free. Cook over low heat for approximately 10 minutes while frequently stirring until heated through.

In the meantime, in a second pan, combine the shredded chicken with the BBQ sauce. Over moderate to low heat, cook until heated through, for approximately 10 minutes, while occasionally stirring.

When you are ready to assemble, arrange the tostada shells on ungreased baking sheets.

Spread the shells with baked beans, and top with the chicken mixture and shredded Cheddar cheese.

Broil around 3-4" away from the heat until the shells are gently browned, and the cheese is entirely melted. This will take approximately 1-2 minutes.

Top with the slaw and serve at once.

Bean, Bacon, and Sausage Hand Pies

You won't have to call your family to the table twice when you bake these perfect pies.

Servings: 12

Total Time: 35mins

Ingredients:

- 6 chipolatas
- 8 strips streaky bacon (diced)
- 1½ (14½ ounces) cans baked beans
- 2 sheets store-bought puff pastry
- 1¾ ounces Cheddar cheese (grated)
- 1 egg (beaten)

Directions:

Arrange the chipolatas on a lined baking sheet and on high heat, grill for 6-8 minutes, turning them over halfway through cooking. Dice the chipolatas into ½ "pieces and put to one side.

In a nonstick frying pan, fry the bacon until just crisp and the fat rendered.

Add the baked beans to the pan, followed by the chipolata.

Next, stir the mixture and bring to a simmer, reducing the sauce a little.

Remove the pan from the heat and set aside to cool completely.

Cut out 24 rounds from the pastry (12 small and 12 large).

Grease a 12-cup muffin pan and push the large rounds into the cups.

Next, spoon approximately 2 tablespoons of the bean mixture into the pastry cups.

Scatter over a little grated Cheddar cheese and brush the exposed pastry with the beaten egg.

Place the small pastry round over the filling, and press gently to seal.

Then, using a cocktail stick, create a small hole in the top of each pie.

Bake the pies in the oven for 15 minutes, and bake at 395 degrees F.

Beef and Baked Bean Cottage Pie

Baked beans add a rich tomato flavor to a classic cottage pie, which is the perfect complement to minced beef.

Servings: 8

Total Time: 1hour 10mins

Ingredients:

Topping:

- 2 pounds potatoes (peeled and coarsely grated)
- 3 tbsp butter
- ¾ cup full-fat cream milk
- Salt and freshly ground black pepper (to season)
- 1 bunch fresh parsley (chopped, to garnish)

Sauce:

- 3 tbsp olive oil (divided)
- 1 pound 2 ounces lean mince beef
- 1 large brown onion (peeled and finely diced)
- 4 large cloves garlic (peeled and crushed
- 2 large carrots (trimmed and diced small)
- 1 pound white mushrooms (sliced)
- ⅓ ounce dried thyme leaves (divided)
- ¼ cup Worcestershire sauce
- 1 (19½ ounces) can baked beans
- 1 cup liquid beef stock
- 1 pound frozen peas
- Salt and freshly ground black pepper (to season)

Directions:

Preheat the main oven to 390 degrees F.

First, make the mash topping. Add the potatoes to a large, deep-sided pan of cold water. Bring to a boil, and cook until softened, for 10-15 minutes.

In the meantime, prepare the meat sauce. Then, in a large deep-sided skillet over high heat, heat 1 tablespoon of oil.

Add half of the meat to the pan, and cook until browned. Set to one side and cook the remaining meat.

Reduce the heat to moderate, and add the remaining 2 tablespoons of oil.

Next, add the onion, garlic, and carrot and fry until the onions start to soften.

Add the mushrooms to the pan. Then, cook until starting to soften.

Return the browned meat to the pan, and add 1 teaspoon of thyme, Worcestershire sauce, baked beans, liquid beef stock, and frozen peas. Mix thoroughly to combine and season generously with salt and freshly ground black pepper.

Cook the mixture for approximately 10-15 minutes, until the sauce starts to thicken.

Once the potatoes are fork-tender, drain well, add the butter, and mash.

Gradually, add the milk and continue mashing until creamy and lump-free.

Taste and season the mash with salt and black pepper. Put to one side.

Transfer the meat mixture to a large deep ovenproof casserole dish.

Top the meat with the mash, fluffing with a fork, and creating an even layer.

Scatter over the remaining thyme and bake in the preheated oven until bubbling and golden.

Garnish with chopped parsley and serve.

Beefy Bean Meatloaf

If you've got lots of hungry mouths to feed, then you need to serve a hearty main, and this beefy bean meatloaf will fit the bill!

Servings: 6-8

Total time: 1hour 5mins

Ingredients:

- 1 onion (peeled and finely chopped)
- 2 cloves garlic (peeled and crushed)
- Splash of oil
- 8 ¾ ounces minced beef
- 16 ounces sausage meat
- ½ cup fresh breadcrumbs
- 1 (14½ ounces) can baked beans
- 1 tbsp Worcestershire sauce
- ½ tsp dried thyme
- 1 handful fresh parsley (finely chopped)
- 2 tbsp tomato sauce
- Mashed potato (to serve, optional)
- Vegetables of choice (to serve, optional)

Directions:

Lightly grease a 9x6" loaf pan. Preheat the main oven to 355 degrees F.

In a pan, over moderate heat, cook the onion along with the garlic in a splash of oil. When the onion is softened, remove the pan from the heat. Transfer the mixture to a bowl to cool.

Add the minced beef, sausage meat, breadcrumbs, baked beans, Worcestershire sauce, dried thyme, and parsley to the bowl, and mix thoroughly to combine.

Next, transfer the meat mixture to the loaf pan, and press the mixture gently but firmly into the pan. Smooth the surface of the mixture and cover the pan with aluminum foil.

Bake the meatloaf in the preheated oven for 45 minutes.

Remove the aluminum foil and brush the top of the meatloaf lightly with tomato sauce. Return the meatloaf to the oven. Then, cook for an additional 5 minutes until the top is glazed.

Then, drain off any of the fat residue and set aside to rest in the loaf tin for 10 minutes, to firm, before turning out onto a plate. Slice the meatloaf into even size thick slices.

Serve the meatloaf with creamy mash, veggies, and additional tomato sauce.

Budget Baked Bean Pasta

Are you stuck for something to eat and not a lot in the store-cupboard? Don't stress; this budget lite bite will get you throughout the day.

Servings: 2

Total Time: 20mins

Ingredients:

- 1 (14½ ounces) can baked beans
- 1 (14½ ounces) can diced tomatoes
- 7 ounces fettuccine
- Salt and freshly ground black pepper (to season)
- Cheese (grated, to garnish, optional)

Directions:

Add the beans and tomatoes to a pan and set over moderate to high heat. Bring to boil before reducing to moderate heat. While occasionally stirring, simmer until slightly thickened, for 12 minutes.

Cook the fettuccine, according to the package instructions, and until al dente. Drain the pasta and return to the same pan you used to cook it in.

Fold the bean-tomato mixture into the drained pasta, and toss to incorporate.

Evenly divide the pasta between 2 bowls, and season to taste with salt and freshly ground black pepper.

Garnish with grated cheese and serve.

Cheesy Bean Pastry Pockets

Golden puff pastry pockets filled with cheesy beans are a quick and easy after-school meal. Serve with a salad for a healthy option.

Servings: 8

Total Time: 25mins

Ingredients:

- 1 (14½ ounces) can baked beans
- 2 ounces Cheddar cheese (finely grated)
- 2 sheets store-bought ready-rolled puff pastry (cut into 8 squares)
- 1 egg (beaten)

Directions:

Preheat the main oven to 355 degrees F.

On the stovetop, heat the baked beans with the cheese.

Add a spoonful of the bean-cheese mixture to the center of each puff pastry square, and fold to create a triangular shape pocket. Using a metal fork, seal the pastry layers.

Brush the tops of the pockets lightly with beaten egg and bake in the preheated oven until golden.

Serve and enjoy.

Chili Bean Tortilla Soup

There is a lot of flavor in a bowl of this Mexican-inspired soup. What's more, it tastes and looks way better than any you can buy in the store.

Servings: 2

Total Time: 20mins

Ingredients:

- Splash of oil
- ½ onion (peeled and chopped)
- 1 tbsp chipotle pepper paste
- 1 freshly squeezed juiced lime
- 1 (14½ ounces) can baked beans
- ½ -1 (14½ ounces) can diced tomatoes
- ½ cup reduced-salt vegetable stock
- ½ tbsp sour cream
- Tortilla chips (crushed, to garnish)

Directions:

heat a splash of oil in a pan.

Add the onion to the pan, and cook until browned.

Next to the pan, add the chipotle pepper paste and lime juice.

Add the baked beans, followed by half of the canned tomatoes and the vegetable stock. Add more canned tomatoes, according to taste. Bring the soup to a boil.

Lastly, serve with a swirl of sour cream and a scattering of crushed tortilla chips.

Coq Au Vin with Baked Beans

French cuisine and baked beans aren't four little words that generally go well together. But when you prepare this recipe, you will be pleasantly surprised at just how well they do!

Servings: 4-6

Total Time: 1hour 50mins

Ingredients:

- 2 tbsp olive oil
- 2 pounds chicken pieces
- Salt and freshly ground black pepper (to season)
- 2 sticks celery (trimmed and chopped)
- 8 shallots
- 3 strips smoky bacon (chopped)
- 5 ounces button mushrooms
- 1 cup red wine
- 1 cup chicken stock
- 2 bay leaves
- 2 tsp fresh thyme sprigs
- 1 (14½ ounces) can baked beans

Directions:

Preheat the main oven to 320 degrees f. Over moderate to high heat, heat the oil.

Season the chicken with salt and black pepper and add them to the pan. Brown the chicken all over on all sides. Remove the chicken from the pan and transfer to a casserole dish.

Add the celery, shallots, and bacon to the pan and cook until golden, for 3-4 minutes.

Add the mushrooms to the pan and cook for an additional 2-3 minutes.

Pour in the red wine, followed by the chicken stock. Add the bay leaves and thyme, and bring to boil. Transfer the mixture to the casserole dish.

Place the dish in the oven. Then, cook for 60-75 minutes, until the meat is tender and is about to fall easily off the bone.

Stir in the baked beans, return to the oven and cook for 15 minutes, until warmed through.

Serve and enjoy.

Country Ham and Bean Stew

Pop these ingredients in your slow cooker, and seven hours later, hey presto, dinner is ready to serve.

Servings: 6

Total Time: 7hours 5mins

Ingredients:

- 2 (14½ ounces) cans baked beans
- 2 medium potatoes (peeled and cut into cubes)
- 2 cups fully cooked, country-style ham (cut into cubes)
- 1 celery rib (trimmed and chopped)
- ½ cup water
- Cheese (grated, to garnish, optional)

Directions:

In a slow cooker of 3-quart capacity, combine the baked beans with the potatoes, ham, celery rib, and water. Mix thoroughly to combine.

Cover with a lid and cook on LOW until the potatoes are fork-tender, for approximately 7 hours.

Garnish with cheese and serve.

Hot Dog Pie

It's time to get creative with some simple store-cupboard ingredients and surprise your family and friends with this great-tasting pie!

Servings: 6

Total Time: 35mins

Ingredients:

- 8 ounces ground beef
- 4 hot dogs (cut lengthwise in half and sliced)
- 1 (14½ ounces) can baked beans
- 2 tbsp brown sugar (to taste)
- ½ cup ketchup
- 2 tbsp prepared mustard
- 2 ounces processed cheese (cut into cubes)
- 1 (9") store-bought, deep-dish pastry shell
- 4 slices American cheese

Directions:

First, in a large pan, over moderate heat, cook the beef until no pink remains. Drain well.

Add the hot dogs followed by the baked beans, brown sugar, ketchup, prepared mustard, and cheese cubes. Cook while stirring until the cheese is entirely melted.

In the meantime, using a fork, prick the pastry shell.

Next, bake the pie in the oven at 400 degrees F for 10 minutes.

Fill the pie with the hot meat mixture.

Then, cut each slice of cheese into 4 strips and create a lattice-style topping over the pie.

Bake in the oven for an additional 5-10 minutes until the cheese is melted.

Lamb and Bean Casserole

Bulk up a meaty casserole with a can of baked beans, and watch those plates clear.

Servings: 4

Total Time: 1hour 25mins

Ingredients:

- 1½ pounds lamb stewing steak (cut into cubes)
- 2¾ tbsp seasoned flour
- ¾ ounce butter
- 4 tomatoes (skinned and cut into quarters)
- 2 onions (peeled, halved, and sliced)
- 2 cups boiling vegetable stock (made using 1 stock cube)
- 2 bay leaves
- 1 tsp dried thyme
- 1 (14½ ounces) can baked beans

Directions:

Add the lamb to a bowl, and toss with the seasoned flour.

In a flameproof casserole dish, melt the butter.

Fry the seasoned lamb in the butter until browned all over.

Add the tomatoes and onions and cook for 1-2 minutes.

Pour in the vegetable stock and add the bay leaves and dried thyme. Bring to a boil while stirring.

Cove the dish with lid, and simmer for 60 minutes, until the meat is fork-tender.

Stir in the baked beans, and cook until heated through for 3-4 minutes.

Meat-Free Baked Bean Meatball Sub

Go meat-free with this baked bean meatball sub. It's the perfect lunchtime lite bite.

Servings: 1

Total Time: 20mins

Ingredients:

- 1 (14½ ounces) can baked beans
- 1 onion (peeled and diced)
- 1 roasted red pepper
- Tomato passata (as needed)
- Breadcrumbs (as needed)
- 1 ounce mozzarella (grated)
- Sub roll (split and toasted)

Directions:

Preheat the main oven to 355 degrees F.

Drain the sauce from the beans, and put it aside.

In a bowl, combine the drained beans with the onion and roasted red pepper.

Add a sufficient amount of tomato passata and breadcrumbs to create a suitable consistency for forming balls.

Form the mixture into balls and arrange in a single layer on a baking sheet. Bake the balls in the preheated oven for 10-15 minutes, or until cooked through and browned.

Sprinkle the mozzarella on the bottom half of the roll and toast both halves of the sub roll.

Place the meat-free meatballs on top of the melted cheese, add a small amount of baked bean sauce. Top with the remaining roll half and enjoy.

New England-Inspired Baked Bean Soup

Baked bean soup is a New England classic, and this recipe featuring canned baked beans gives the hearty soup a modern makeover.

Servings: 6-8

Total Time: 30mins

Ingredients:

- 6 cups cold water
- 1 (14½ ounces) can diced tomatoes
- 2 stalks celery (trimmed and diced)
- 1 small onion (peeled and diced)
- 2 (14½ ounces) cans baked beans (divided)
- ¼ cup light brown sugar
- 1 tbsp hot sauce
- Salt and freshly ground pepper (to season)
- Crusty bread (to serve, optional)

Directions:

In a large pan, set over moderate heat, combine the water with the tomatoes, celery, and onion. Set 1 cup of cold beans aside and add the remaining beans to the mixture. Bring the mixture to a boil, turn the heat down and simmer for approximately 5 minutes.

Transfer the mixture to a food blender, and puree to a soup consistency. Return the soup to the pan, and bring back to a simmer.

Add the remaining 1 cup of baked beans, brown sugar, and hot sauce. Taste and season the mixture with salt and black pepper, and simmer for another 15 minutes.

Serve with crusty bread and enjoy.

Pizza Margherita with Baked Beans

Quick and easy, this delicious pizza made with four simple ingredients is an ideal meal for kids.

Servings: 2

Total Time: 25mins

Ingredients:

- 3 tbsp store-bought tomato pizza sauce
- 1 (9") pizza base
- 1 (14½ ounces) can baked beans
- 1½ cups mozzarella cheese (freshly grated)

Directions:

Preheat the main oven to 375 degrees F.

Spread the tomato base evenly over the pizza base.

Spoon the baked beans over the base. You may not need to use the whole can.

Scatter the grated mozzarella cheese over the beans.

Bake the pizza in the oven for approximately 15-20 minutes, until hot.

Serve and enjoy.

Potato-Topped Meatballs and Baked Beans

Make a meal of frozen meatballs and three varieties of beans with this potato topped pie.

Servings: 6

Total Time: 1hour 5mins

Ingredients:

- Nonstick cooking spray
- 1 (14½ ounces) can baked beans (undrained)
- 1 (14½ ounces) can red kidney beans (drained and rinsed)
- 1½ cups frozen cut beans
- ½ cup frozen onion (peeled and chopped)
- ¼ cup store-bought BBQ sauce
- 5 ounces frozen, cooked Italian meatballs
- 1 cup shoestring potatoes

Directions:

First, preheat the main oven to 375 degrees F.

Second, spray a casserole dish of 2-quart capacity with nonstick cooking spray.

In the casserole dish, combine the baked beans with the kidney beans, frozen cut beans, frozen onion, BBQ sauce, and meatballs. Mix thoroughly to combine and cover with a lid.

Next, bake the casserole in the oven for 30 minutes.

Remove the lid, and scatter the shoestring potatoes over the top. Press the potatoes down lightly and bake in the oven, uncovered for another 20-25 minutes, until heated through and bubbling.

Skillet Saltfish, Veggies and Baked Beans

Serve this fishy feast with rice or baby potatoes. It's a favorite Jamaican combo.

Servings: 2

Total Time: 8hours 55mins

Ingredients:

- 6 ounces saltfish
- 4 cups water
- 3 plum tomatoes
- 1 onion (peeled)
- 1 tsp Scotch bonnet pepper
- 2 stalks scallion
- 3 tbsp vegetable oil
- ½ tsp freshly ground black pepper
- 1 small sweet red pepper
- 1 sprig thyme
- 1 (14½ ounces) can baked beans

Directions:

Soak the catfish overnight. Remove from the water, pat dry, remove the bones and flake the fish into small pieces.

Chop the plum tomatoes, onion, Scotch bonnet, and scallion.

In a skillet, heat the oil.

Add the seasoning to the pan and along with the red pepper and thyme. Add the plum tomatoes, onion, Scotch bonnet, and scallion mixture. Sauté for approximately 60 seconds.

Add the saltfish flakes to the mixture, followed by the baked beans. Season the mixture with freshly ground black pepper. Stir thoroughly to combine and cook for an additional 60 seconds.

Serve and enjoy.

Slow-Cooked Paprika Pork, Beans, and Roasted Tomatoes

This tempting main meal cooked low and slow is a real weekend treat.

Servings: 4

Total Time: 2hours

Ingredients:

- 1 tbsp extra-virgin olive oil
- 1 onion (peeled and chopped)
- 1 clove garlic (peeled and crushed)
- 2 tsp smoked paprika
- 2 pounds pork shoulder
- 1 (14½ ounces) can baked beans
- 2 handfuls grape tomatoes (left whole)
- Splash of red wine vinegar
- Splash of water (as needed)
- 4 handfuls baby spinach
- 1 tsp fresh parsley (chopped)

Directions:

In a casserole dish, heat the oil.

Add the onion, garlic, and paprika. Then, cook until the onions are just golden. Add the pork shoulder and brown all over.

Stir in the baked beans, and add the whole grape tomatoes, followed by a splash of vinegar and a splash of water. Simmer over low heat for 2 hours until the meats pull apart.

Fold in the spinach and garnish with chopped parsley.

Serve and enjoy.

Slow Cooker Chicken and Baked Bean Casserole

If you are watching your weight or looking for a healthy main, this slow cooker casserole recipe is the one for you. It has lots of protein and fresh veggies and is packed full of taste, thanks to its seasoning blend.

Servings: 4

Total Time: 4hours 15mins

Ingredients:

- 4 boneless skinless chicken breasts (cut into medium size chunks)
- 1 onion (peeled and finely sliced)
- 2 cloves garlic (peeled and crushed)
- 14 ounces baby carrots
- 14 ounces baby new potatoes (halved or quartered)
- 1 (14½ ounces) can baked beans
- 2 cups chicken stock
- 3 tbsp smoked paprika
- 1 tsp dried basil
- 1 tsp oregano
- Pinch of salt
- Dash of freshly ground black pepper
- Fresh Italian parsley (chopped, to garnish)

Directions:

Add all the ingredients to a slow cooker in recipe order (chicken, onion, garlic, carrots, new potatoes, baked beans, chicken stock paprika, dried basil, oregano, salt, and pepper). Stir gently to combine.

Cover and cook on LOW for 8 hours or on HIGH for 4 hours.

Serve and enjoy garnished with chopped parsley.

Spanish-Style Baked Bean Omelet

A delicious omelet packed full of protein-rich eggs and cheese, and flavorful bacon, sweet and tangy baked beans makes a healthy lite bite or main.

Servings: 2-4

Total Time: 25mins

Ingredients:

- 6 eggs (room temperature)
- 2 tbsp water
- 1 tbsp extra-virgin olive oil
- 1 Spanish red onion (peeled and finely chopped)
- 4 strips bacon (rind-free, thinly sliced crosswise)
- 1 red capsicum (thinly sliced)
- 2 zucchinis (grated)
- 1 (8 ounces) can baked beans
- ⅓ cup Cheddar cheese (grated)
- 2 Turkish white rolls (split, toasted, buttered, and sliced into thick fingers)

Directions:

In a jug, whisk the eggs with 2 tablespoons of water, and put aside.

Over high heat, heat the oil in a skillet.

Add the onion to the skillet followed by the bacon and red capsicum, and while stirring, cook for 5 minutes, until golden.

Add the zucchini to the skillet and cook while stirring until softened, for 2 minutes.

Take the pan off the heat. Then, stir in the baked beans.

Return the pan to medium heat. Pour in the egg mixture, tilting the pan to make sure the base is evenly covered. Scatter with the grated cheese.

As the omelet begins to set, using a spatula, lift the omelet around the edges, so the uncooked egg runs underneath and cooks. Continue to cook for a few minutes until the base of the omelet is set and golden.

Cover the pan with a lid. Then, cook for an additional 60 seconds until set.

Transfer the omelet to a heatproof board, and cut into wedges.

Serve the omelet with toasted bread fingers.

Spicy Baked Bean Tuna Toast Topper

You will be surprised at just how well baked beans pair with tuna to create the perfect protein-packed toast topper.

Servings: 4-6

Total Time: 30mins

Ingredients:

- 2-3 tbsp sunflower oil
- 1 onion (peeled and sliced)
- 1 sprig curry leaves
- 2 cloves garlic (peeled and grated)
- ½ tsp ground red chili powder
- ½ tsp freshly ground black pepper
- ¼ - ½ Scotch bonnet pepper
- 1 tsp tomato paste
- 1 (14¾ ounces) can tuna in spring water
- 1 (14½ ounces) can baked beans
- Salt (to season)
- Toast (buttered, to serve, optional)

Directions:

Heat the oil in a pan.

Add the onion to the pan and cook until translucent and softened.

Add the curry leaves and garlic and sauté for 60 seconds.

Add the red chili powder, black pepper, and the Scotch bonnet (left whole so you can remove it from the pan if the mixture is becoming overly spicy).

Stir in the tomato paste to combine.

Add a splash of water, approximately ¼ cup, to prevent the spices from burning.

Flake the canned tuna, using a fork, and stir into the mixture to combine.

Add the baked beans, season with salt to taste, and stir to incorporate.

Cover the pan, and cook until the mixture is thickened and bubbling.

Serve and enjoy on slices of lightly buttered toast.

Spicy Baked Bean Jambalaya

Add a taste of the south to your dinner table with this quick and easy spicy jambalaya. Let the good times roll!

Servings: 4-6

Total Time: 35mins

Ingredients:

- 1 tsp canola oil
- 2 cups frozen garden vegetables
- 8 ounces spicy Italian sausage (sliced)
- 1 cup ham (cubed)
- 2 (14½ ounces) cans chopped tomatoes
- 1 cup chicken stock
- 1 cup long-grain white rice
- 12 jumbo shrimps (peeled and deveined)
- 1 (14½ ounces) can baked beans
- Louisiana hot sauce (to taste)

Directions:

First, in a large pan, heat the oil to moderate to high heat.

Sauté the garden veggies for 2 minutes.

Add the sausage meat and ham to the pan, and cook for an additional 2-3 minutes.

Add the canned tomatoes and pour in the chicken stock, and bring to a boil.

Stir in the rice, reduce the heat to moderate to low and while covered, cook for 20 minutes.

Then, add the jumbo shrimp and the baked beans. Stir and while covered, cook until the rice is tender.

Serve the jambalaya with a splash of Louisiana hot sauce.

Steak and Baked Bean Stroganoff Pie

Undoubtedly, this tasty meal is sure to become a new family favorite. It combines all the meaty flavor of stroganoff in a wholesome and comforting pie.

Servings: 6

Total Time: 55mins

Ingredients:

- 2 tbsp olive oil (divided)
- 16 ounces beef rump steak (thinly sliced)
- Pinch of salt and freshly ground black pepper (to season)
- 1 large brown onion (peeled and diced small)
- 3 cloves garlic (peeled and finely chopped)
- 7 ounces white mushrooms (thinly sliced)
- 1 tsp Dijon mustard
- 1 cup liquid beef stock
- 2 tbsp Worcestershire sauce
- 1 (19½ ounces) can baked beans
- 2 tbsp sour cream
- 1 package store-bought filo pastry (thawed)
- 2 tbsp butter (melted)

Directions:

Preheat the main oven to 390 degrees F.

Over moderate to high heat, heat a large skillet. Add 1 tablespoon of oil to the pan and cook the steak until caramelized. You may need to do this in batches. Season the cooked meat with salt and black pepper and set aside in a bowl.

Next, in the same pan, add another tablespoon of oil and cook the onion, garlic, and mushrooms until softened, for 2-3 minutes.

Add the Dijon mustard, beef stock, Worcestershire sauce, and baked beans. Season the mixture with salt and black pepper, and stir to combine.

Return the meat to the pan, along with its juices, and cook on moderate heat for 60 seconds, until thoroughly combined.

Take the pan off the heat. Then, gently stir in the sour cream.

Transfer the meat mixture to a pie dish.

Next, prepare the pastry. Unroll the thawed pastry and one sheet of pastry at a time, scrunch up and place on top of the filling. Add the pastry until its entire surface is evenly covered.

Then, brush the pastry with melted butter and bake in the preheated oven for 25-30 minutes, or until the pastry is crunchy and golden brown.

Serve and enjoy.

The Big Breakfast Baked Bean Bake

Hash browns, bacon, mushrooms, baked beans, and eggs topped off with a grated cheese garnish. This bake has to be the best big breakfast ever!

Servings: 4

Total Time: 30mins

Ingredients:

- 6-8 frozen hash browns
- Splash of oil
- 1 onion (peeled and finely chopped)
- 4 slices bacon
- 3½ ounces button mushrooms (sliced)
- 1 (14½ ounces) can baked beans
- 4 eggs
- ¼ cup Cheddar cheese (grated)
- Fresh parsley (chopped, to garnish)

Directions:

First, preheat the main oven to 400 degrees F.

Arrange the frozen hash browns in a single layer in an 8" square baking dish and bake in the preheated oven for 15 minutes.

In the meantime, prepare the filling. Over moderate heat, in a skillet or frying pan, heat a splash of oil.

Add the onion and bacon to the skillet and sauté until the bacon is cooked and the onion softened.

Next, add the mushrooms and continue to cook for an additional 60 seconds.

Add the baked beans to the pan, and stir while they heat through.

Spoon the mixture over the hash browns.

Then, using the back of a spoon, create 4 wells on the surface of the mixture.

Break the eggs into the indents, and sprinkle over the grated Cheddar cheese.

Cover the dish lightly with a sheet of aluminum foil, ensuring it does not contact the eggs.

Return the dish to the oven. Then, bake for an additional 10-15 minutes, until the eggs are set to your preferred level of doneness.

Garnish with chopped parsley and serve.

Veggie Cowboy Pie

Not all cowboys are meat eaters! And this veggie pie will feed a family after a hard day in the great outdoors.

Servings: 4

Total Time: 40mins

Ingredients:

- 8 vegetarian sausages
- 3 large potatoes (peeled and boiled)
- 2 tbsp milk
- 1 tbsp butter
- 1 onion (peeled and chopped)
- 2 (14½ ounces) cans baked beans
- 1 ounce cheese (freshly grated)

Directions:

Preheat your grill to 390 degrees F.

Arrange the sausages on a baking tray and grill until golden and cooked through on all sides.

Mash the boiled potatoes, add the milk and butter to make a creamy mash.

Over high heat, in a skillet, fry the onion until golden.

Add the beans to a large ovenproof casserole dish. Add the sausages and onion to the dish.

Top with an even layer of creamy mash potatoes.

Scatter the grated cheese over the mash, followed by the thyme.

Grill the pie until the cheese is golden and the filling is beginning to bubble.

Sides

Baked Bean Fritters

These fritters make a crisp and tasty snack or side. Serve with slices of fresh tomato and a rocket salad.

Servings: 4

Total Time: 25mins

Ingredients:

- Splash of oil
- ½ onion (peeled and chopped)
- 2 strips bacon (diced)
- 1 (14½ ounces) can baked beans
- 2 tbsp fresh parsley (chopped)
- ¾ cup leftover mashed potato (cold)
- ½ cup self-raising flour
- 2 eggs (separated)
- Salt and freshly ground black pepper
- Sliced tomato (to serve, optional)
- Rocket salad (to serve, optional)

Directions:

Heat a splash of oil in a skillet or frying pan.

Add the onion together with the bacon to the pan and fry gently until tender but not browned.

In a bowl, combine the baked beans with the cooked onion, bacon, parsley, leftover mash, flour, and egg yolks. Then, mix thoroughly and season with salt and black pepper.

In a bowl, beat the egg whites until stiffened. Fold the egg white carefully into the bean mixture using a large metal spoon.

Heat a drop of oil in the frying pan, and over low to moderate heat, cook large spoonfuls of the mixture for approximately 3 minutes on each side. Keep the mixture warm in the oven until all of it is cooked.

Serve the baked beans fritters with slices of fresh tomato and rocket salad.

Baked Bean Mexican-Style Stuffed Bell Peppers

If you are planning a tasty Mexican-style main, why not push the boat out and accompany it with this sensational side dish!

Servings: 4-8

Total Time: 1hour 15mins

Ingredients:

- 4 large green bell peppers
- 1 (8 ounces) can baked beans
- 1 (11 ounces) can Mexican-style corn (drained)
- ¼ cup onion (peeled and finely chopped)
- 1 clove garlic (peeled and minced)
- 2 fresh jalapenos (chopped)
- ¼ tsp cumin
- ¼ cup cilantro (chopped)
- Salt and freshly ground black pepper (to season)
- 1 cup water
- 6 ounces Pepper Jack cheese (shredded)

Directions:

First, prepare the bell peppers. You can do this by cutting them lengthwise in half, removing the seeds but leaving the stem in place.

Arrange the pepper halves, cut side facing upwards on a 13x8" baking pan.

In a bowl, combine the baked beans with the Mexican corn, onion, garlic, jalapenos, cumin, cilantro, salt, and black pepper. Mix lightly to incorporate.

Spoon approximately ¼ cup of the filling into each bell pepper.

Pour the water into the baking pan to surround the halves of pepper.

Cover the pan tightly with aluminum foil and bake in the oven at 350 degrees F, until the peppers are softened, for 45-50 minutes.

Take the pan out of the oven, and garnish with shredded Pepper Jack cheese.

Return the pan to the oven for a few minutes to allow the cheese to melt.

Serve and enjoy.

BBQ Baked Beans

These BBQ beans are hard to beat. Serve them at your next get-together or potluck, and watch them disappear!

Servings: 6-8

Total Time: 55mins

Ingredients:

- 2 (14½ ounces) cans baked beans (drained)
- 2 medium tart apples (peeled, cored, and chopped)
- 1 onion (peeled and coarsely chopped)
- 1 cup store-bought BBQ sauce
- ⅓ cup packed brown sugar
- 1 jalapeno pepper (seeded and chopped)
- ½ cup raisins
- 3 strips bacon (diced)

Directions:

In a large bowl, combine the baked beans with the apple, onion, BBQ sauce, brown sugar, jalapeno, and raisins.

Transfer the bean mixture to an 11x7" casserole dish.

Scatter the diced bacon over the top and cover with a lid.

Bake in the oven for 25-30 minutes, until the mixture bubbles and is your preferred consistency.

Serve and enjoy.

Maple Baked Beans

This versatile side can be served at breakfast, lunch, or dinner. They are particularly tasty alongside waffles, bacon, burgers, ribs, and more.

Servings: 10

Total Time: 20mins

Ingredients:

- 1 medium onion (peeled and chopped)
- 1-2 tbsp canola oil
- 6 (14½ ounces) cans baked beans
- 1 ½ tsp ground mustard
- 1 tsp garlic salt
- ¾-1 cup pure maple syrup

Directions:

In a Dutch oven, cook the chopped onion in the canola oil until tender.

Next, add the baked beans, ground mustard, and garlic salt.

Cook over moderate heat, while occasionally stirring, until bubbling.

Add the maple syrup, and while occasionally stirring, heat through.

Serve and enjoy.

Peach Baked Beans

It's official, peach pie filling isn't just a dessert ingredient, so if you are cooking for a sweet-toothed crowd, you will need to serve a hearty portion of these sweet baked beans.

Servings: 8-10

Total Time: 1hour 30mins

Ingredients:

- ½ cup ketchup
- ½ cup pure maple syrup
- ¼ cup Dijon mustard
- 3 cups canned peach pie filling
- 1 tsp apple cider vinegar
- 1 (7 ounces) jar diced pimiento peppers (drained)
- ¼ cup packed light brown sugar
- Sea salt (to season)
- Freshly ground black pepper (to season)
- 4 (14½ ounces) cans baked beans (rinsed and drained)

Directions:

In a pan, combine the ketchup with the maple syrup, Dijon mustard, canned peach pie filling, apple cider vinegar, pimiento pepper, and brown sugar.

Bring the mixture to a boil, whisking continually until the sugar dissolves entirely.

Turn the heat down to medium-low and simmer for approximately 20 minutes until it reduces by one third. Season to taste with salt and freshly ground black pepper.

Preheat the main oven to 325 degrees F.

Pour the sauce and the baked beans into a large casserole dish, and stir well to combine.

Partially cover the dish, and bake in the preheated oven for 60 minutes until the beans are glazed.

Taste, season, and serve.

Ratatouille with Baked Beans

Serve this healthy French-inspired stew with crusty bread or as a side dish to add flavor and color to the main meal.

Servings: 4-6

Total Time: 40mins

Ingredients:

- 2 tbsp extra-virgin olive oil
- 1 red onion (peeled and sliced)
- 2 cloves garlic (peeled and minced or crushed)
- 1 medium eggplant (cut into ¾" chunks)
- 1 red capsicum (cut into chunks)
- 2 zucchinis (cubed)
- 1 tsp rubbed sweet basil
- 1 (14½ ounces) can chopped tomatoes
- Salt and freshly ground black pepper (to season)
- 1 (14½ ounces) can baked beans
- 2 tbsp fresh basil leaves

Directions:

In a large skillet or frying pan, heat the oil over moderate heat.

Add the onion together with the garlic and cook until softened, for 3-4 minutes.

Add the eggplant followed by the red capsicum and zucchini and cook while stirring for 5 minutes.

Add the rubbed sweet basil and tomatoes and season with salt and black pepper.

Bring the mixture to boil, cover with a lid and simmer for 20 minutes until the veggies are fork-tender. You may need to add a drop of water to the skillet to thin out the consistency.

Stir in the baked beans to combine thoroughly and bring to boil before simmering for an additional 1-2 minutes, until warmed.

Garnish with fresh basil leaves and serve.

Slow Cooker Boozy Bourbon Baked Beans with Bacon

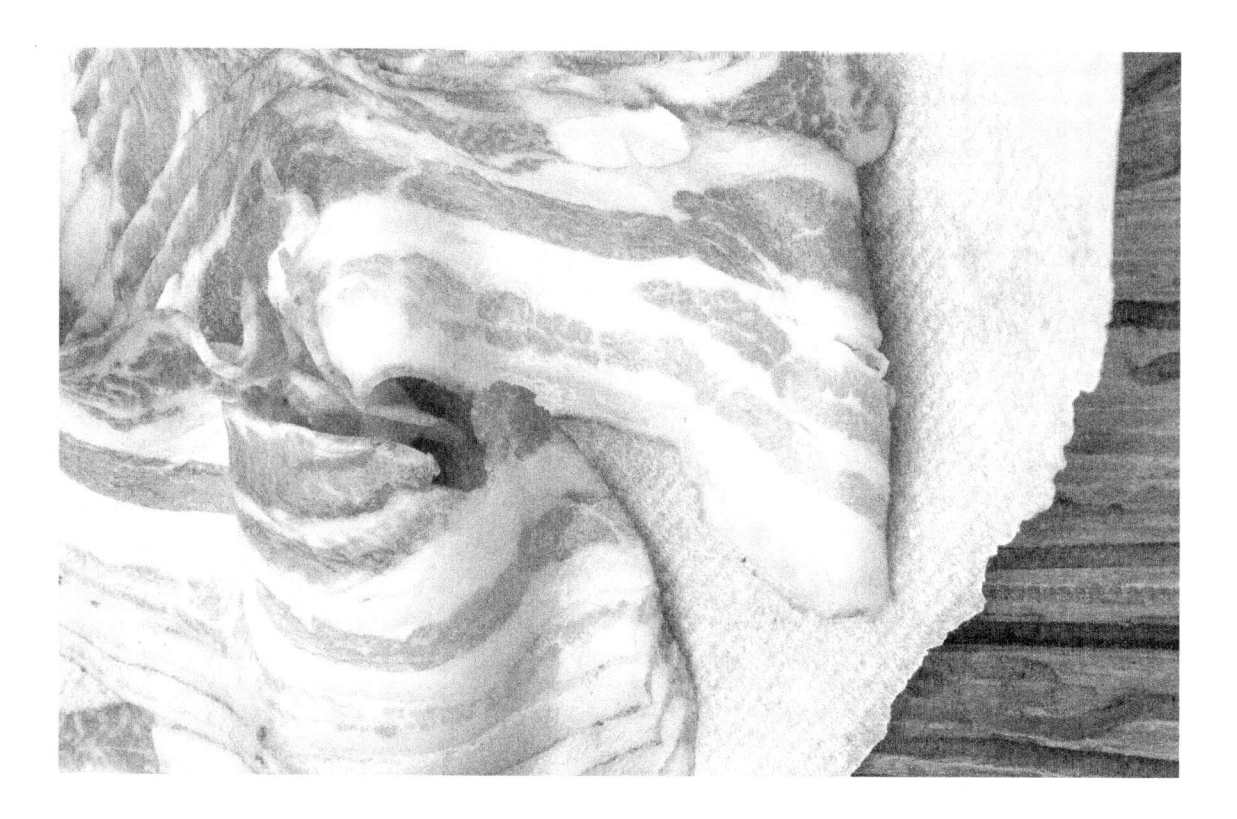

This slow cooker recipe is full of beans, but better yet, it has a large splash of bourbon to give it a boozy boost.

Servings: 15-20

Total Time: 4hours 30mins

Ingredients:

- 6 strips smoked bacon
- 1 cup onion (peeled and chopped)
- 3 (14½ ounces) cans baked beans with pork (undrained)
- 1 (14½ ounces) can Northern beans (drained and rinsed)
- 1 (14½ ounces) can Navy beans (drained and rinsed)
- ¾ cup ketchup
- ¼ cup molasses
- ¼ cup brown sugar
- ¼ cup bourbon
- 2 tbsp yellow mustard
- 1 tbsp Worcestershire sauce
- ½ tsp freshly ground black pepper
- ½ tsp salt
- ¼ tsp garlic powder
- ¼ tsp cayenne pepper

Directions:

Cook the bacon in a skillet or frying pan. When cooked, using a slotted spoon, remove the bacon from the pan and transfer to a kitchen paper towel-lined plate. Leave 1 tablespoon of the bacon drippings in the pan.

Add the onion to the pan, and sauté for 3-4 minutes.

Add the onion, canned baked beans, Northern beans, Navy beans, ketchup, molasses, brown sugar, bourbon, yellow mustard, Worcestershire sauce, salt, cayenne, and garlic powder to a slow cooker of 6-quart capacity. Stir the mixture well, cover with the lid, and on LOW, cook for 4 hours.

Remove the lid from the slow cooker, increase heat to HIGH and cook to thicken for approximately 20 minutes.

Stir in the bacon to combine evenly and serve.

Spicy Beans and Rice

This side dish will have everyone coming back for more. It will add flavor, spice, and a lot more to your next Mexican family-friendly feast.

Servings: 8

Total Time: 25mins

Ingredients:

- 1 cup uncooked instant white rice
- 1 cup water
- 1 tbsp oil
- ¼ cup red onion (peeled and chopped)
- 2 (14½ ounces) cans baked beans
- 1 (4½ ounces) can chopped green chilies
- 1 ounce taco seasoning mix
- ½ cup sour cream
- ½ cup Cheddar cheese (shredded)

Directions:

Cook the instant rice in water as directed on the package instructions.

In the meantime, heat the oil in a pan over moderate to high heat until hot.

Add the onion to the pan, and cook while stirring for 60 seconds. Turn the heat down to moderate.

Add the baked beans, chopped green chilies, and taco seasoning, and mix to combine thoroughly.

Cook the mixture until it just comes to a boil, while occasionally stirring.

Next, add the cooked rice from Step 1, and mix thoroughly.

Transfer to a dish, and serve with sour cream and a sprinkling of shredded Cheddar.

Sweet Corn and Baked Bean Salsa

This sweet and spicy salsa is ready to serve in just a few minutes. What could be a simpler side to feed a hungry crowd?

Servings: 8

Total Time: 5mins

Ingredients:

- 2 (14½ ounces) cans baked beans
- 1 (14½ ounces) can diced tomatoes with jalapeno peppers
- 1 cup canned sweet corn kernels
- Tortilla chips (to serve)

Directions:

In a serving bowl, combine the baked beans with the canned tomatoes and sweet corn.

Serve with tortilla chips and enjoy.

Sweet 'n Sour Beans

Sweet and sour beans are popular throughout the world, and this slow cooker recipe is an easy and fuss-free option.

Servings: 20

Total Time: 3hours 20mins

Ingredients:

- 8 strips bacon (diced)
- 2 medium onions (peeled, halved, and thinly sliced)
- 1 cup packed brown sugar
- ½ cup cider vinegar
- 1 tsp salt
- 1 tsp ground mustard
- ½ tsp garlic powder
- 2 (14½ ounces) cans baked beans (undrained)
- 1 (14½ ounces) can kidney beans (rinsed and drained)
- 1 (14½ ounces) can pinto beans (rinsed and drained)
- 1 (14½ ounces) can lima beans (rinsed and drained)
- 1 (14½ ounces) can black-eyed peas (rinsed and drained)

Directions:

In a large skillet or frying pan, cook the bacon over moderate heat until crispy.

Remove the bacon from the pan and set aside on a plate lined with kitchen paper towels to drain. Put 2 tablespoons of the bacon drippings to one side.

Sauté the onions in the bacon drippings until fork tender.

Next, add the sugar, cider vinegar, salt, ground mustard, and garlic powder, and bring the ingredients to boil.

In a slow cooker of 5-quart capacity, combine the baked beans, kidney beans, pinto beans, lima beans, and black-eyed peas. Add the onion mixture to the beans followed by the bacon, stirring to incorporate thoroughly.

Cover with a lid and on HIGH cook until heated through, for 3-4 hours.

Author's Afterthoughts

thank you

I would like to express my deepest thanks to you, the reader, for making this investment in one my books. I cherish the thought of bringing the love of cooking into your home.

With so much choice out there, I am grateful you decided to Purch this book and read it from beginning to end.

Please let me know by submitting an Amazon review if you enjoyed this book and found it contained valuable information to help you in your culinary endeavors. Please take a few minutes to express your opinion freely and honestly. This will help others make an informed decision on purchasing and provide me with valuable feedback.

Thank you for taking the time to review!

Christina Tosch

About the Author

Christina Tosch is a successful chef and renowned cookbook author from Long Grove, Illinois. She majored in Liberal Arts at Trinity International University and decided to pursue her passion of cooking when she applied to the world renowned Le Cordon Bleu culinary school in Paris, France. The school was lucky to recognize the immense talent of this chef and she excelled in her courses, particularly Haute Cuisine. This skill was recognized and rewarded by several highly regarded Chicago restaurants, where she was offered the prestigious position of head chef.

Christina and her family live in a spacious home in the Chicago area and she loves to grow her own vegetables and herbs in the garden she lovingly cultivates on her sprawling estate. Her and her husband have two beautiful children, 3 cats, 2 dogs and a parakeet they call Jasper. When Christina is not hard at work creating beautiful meals for Chicago's elite, she is hard at work writing engaging e-books of which she has sold over 1500.

Make sure to keep an eye out for her latest books that offer helpful tips, clear instructions and witty anecdotes that will bring a smile to your face as you read!

Printed in Great Britain
by Amazon

80845017R00066